Hello Earth...Here We Come

Nita Ganguly
Illustrated by **Niramoy Ganguly**

RED TURTLE
RUPA

Published in Red Turtle by
Rupa Publications India Pvt. Ltd 2017
7/16, Ansari Road, Daryaganj
New Delhi 110002

Sales centres:
Allahabad Bengaluru Chennai
Hyderabad Jaipur Kathmandu
Kolkata Mumbai

Text Copyright © Nita Ganguly 2017
Illustrations Copyright © Rupa Publications Pvt. Ltd 2017
Photos courtesy Niramoy Ganguly & NASA

The views and opinions expressed in this book are the author's own and the
facts are as reported by her which have been verified to the extent possible,
and the publishers are not in any way liable for the same.

All rights reserved.
No part of this publication may be reproduced, transmitted,
or stored in a retrieval system, in any form or by any means,
electronic, mechanical, photocopying, recording or otherwise,
without the prior permission of the publisher.

ISBN: 978-81-291-4479-9

First impression 2017

10 9 8 7 6 5 4 3 2 1

The moral right of the author has been asserted.

Printed at Lustra Print Process, New Delhi

This book is sold subject to the condition that it shall not,
by way of trade or otherwise, be lent, resold, hired out,
or otherwise circulated, without the publisher's prior consent,
in any form of binding or cover other than that
in which it is published.

To my mother

Nomita Chatterjee

Ma, you are AMAZING...BEAUTIFUL...STRONG...GRACEFUL...WISE...

Absolutely PERFECT.

Your advice has always been GOLD and your support is solid as a ROCK.

What I am today is because of your unconditional LOVE and TRUST

LOVE YOU, MA.

'Een, are we lost?' asked Ali. Een and Ali were travelling in their spaceship and heading towards their chosen holiday destination, Earth.

'No. See that Blue Dot, it is EARTH,' said Een confidently.

'WOW! It looks like a Blue Marble,' Ali said excitedly, seeing Earth more clearly a little later.

'Yes, that's how it looks from a distance!' said Een, sitting at the control panel.

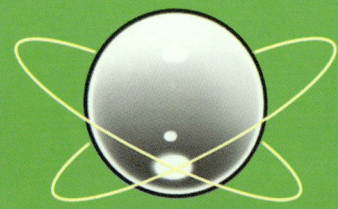

Ali and Een kept looking fixedly at the beautiful planet Earth as it came closer and closer and grew bigger.

'Look! There are other colours too—brown, yellow, green, white… SOOO many of them!' Ali exclaimed.

'Well, the blue part is water, of course. The brown, yellow and green parts are land. The white portions are ice, snow and clouds,' Een proudly explained. He had read a lot about Planet Earth before planning this holiday.

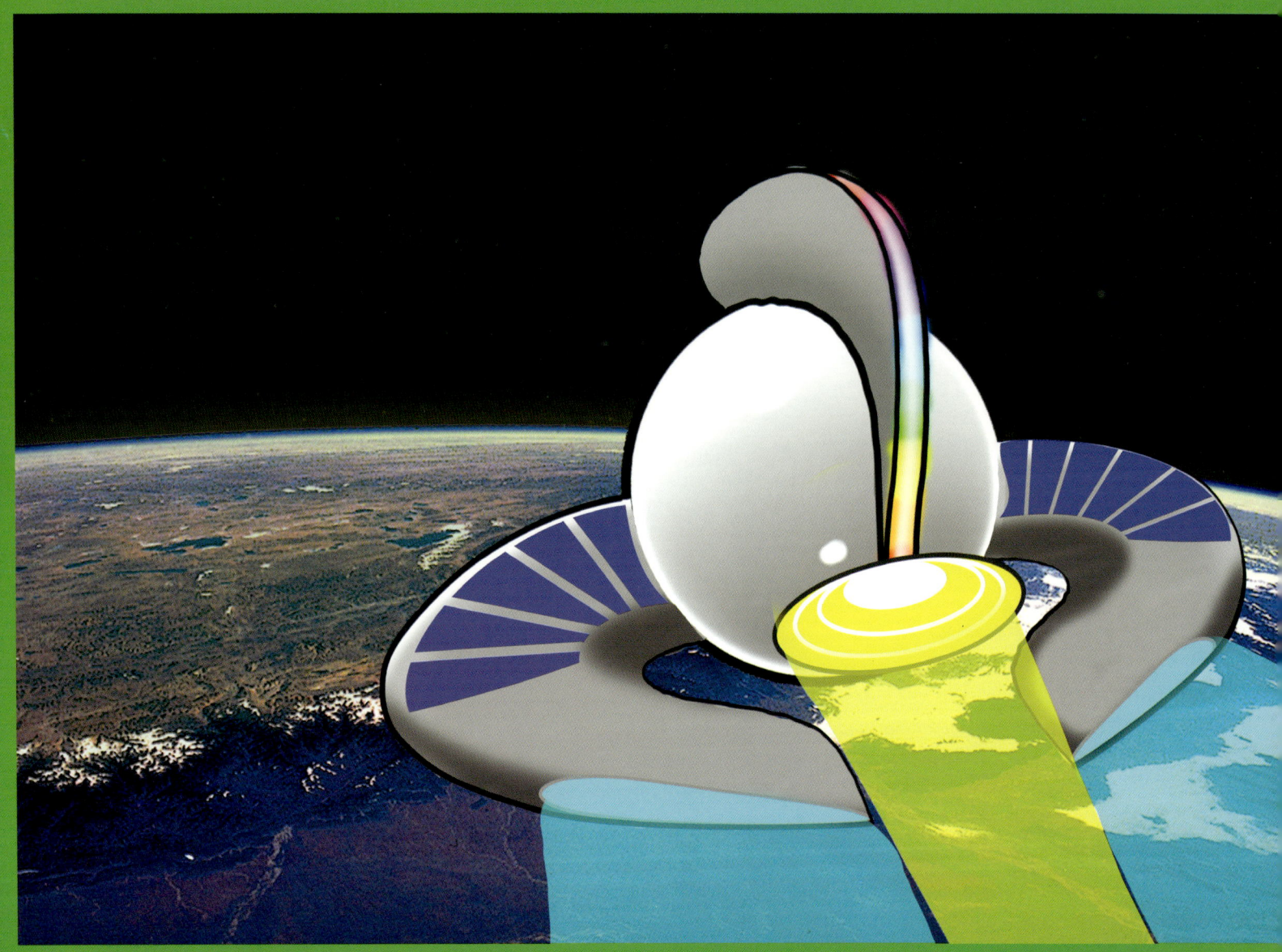

'This place is perfect for a HOLIDAY,' said Ali, thrilled.

'Can't wait to take pictures and share them with my friends back home!' said Een eagerly.

Meanwhile, as their spaceship crossed Earth's moon, Een said, 'We are about to land. Buckle up your seatbelt, Ali. Here we goooo!'

'Yipeeee! Hello Earth...here we come!' cried Ali. 'Do we need to wear a mask?' he asked as they were about to touch ground.

'No! Not at all. Earth has plenty of oxygen and the air is clean and fresh,' said Een as the spaceship touched down.

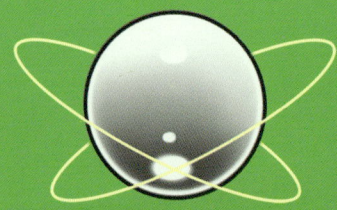

Ali and Een took their backpack and camera and stepped out of the spaceship, looking around with curiosity. However, they were uneasy in no time.

'Ahm! I feel a little funny and my eyes are burning,' said Ali.

'Me too! I feel choked,' said Een, coughing. 'Let's get inside our spaceship.'

They turned on their heels and rushed to their spaceship, gasping for breath, and closed the door of the spaceship.

'Are you sure this is Earth?' asked Ali. 'The air outside is so polluted!'

'Maybe we are at the wrong spot. Let's explore ahead,' said Een.

But they were unable to find another place to land. Instead, Een soon saw rows of tall chimneys ahead. 'Look! That's where the polluting SMOKE is coming from,' he pointed out.

Ali looked horrified and cried, 'Ufff! Clouds of dirty air are everywhere. Why can't they just use clean energy in their factories?'

Een steered the spaceship a little further. Next, to their shock, they saw a vast traffic jam. Many humans were moving in their vehicles with difficulty, honking endlessly.

'This is double trouble. It's SMOKY and NOISY out here,' said Een, shaking his head, disappointed. 'Have they not heard of SOLAR ENERGY? It's free and clean.'

Ali grumbled, 'Een, let's go from here. I want to start my holiday.'

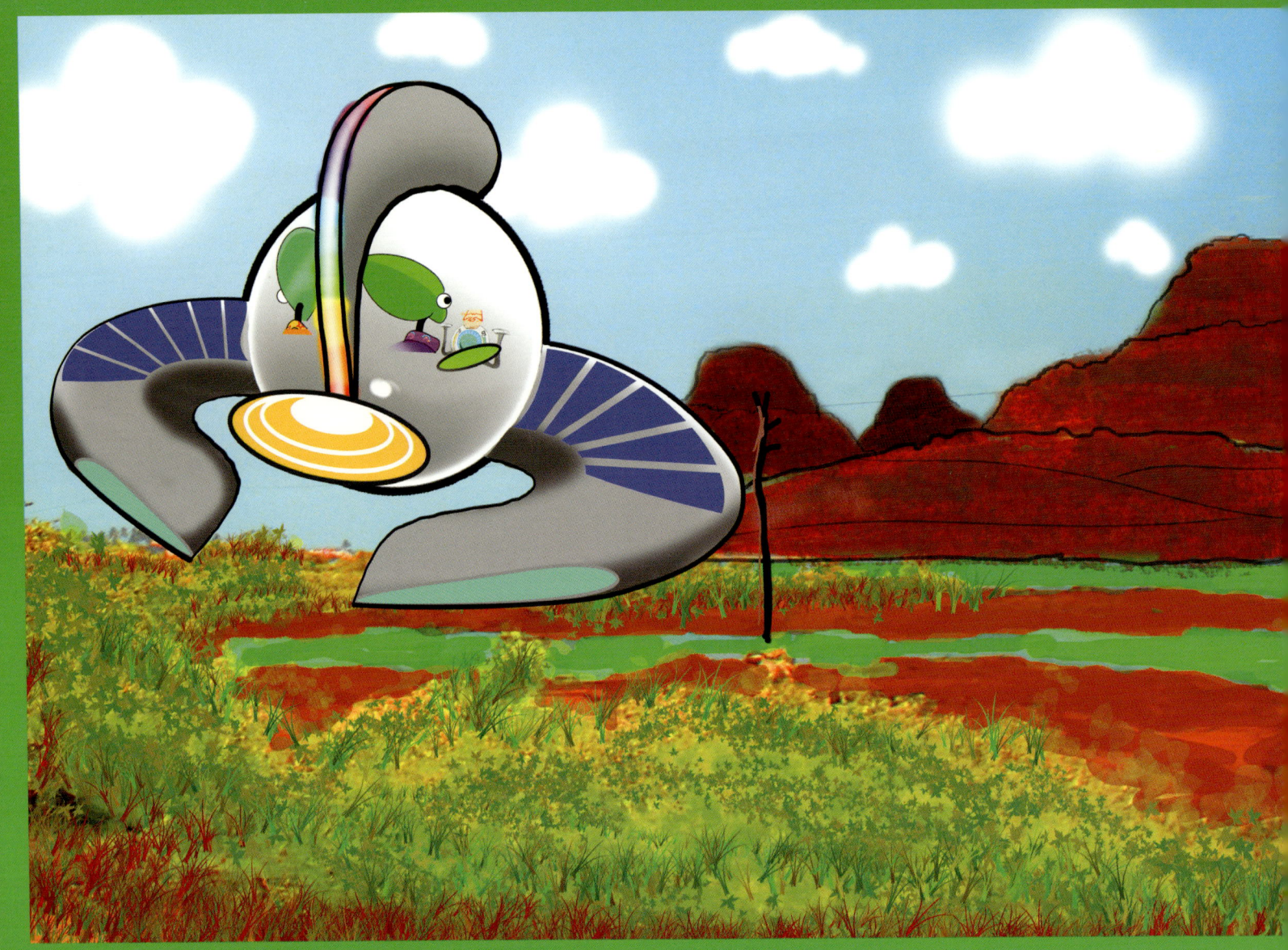

Een knew about his friend's nature so he did not argue. He flew a little higher to get a better view of a suitable place to land the spaceship. He soon found one.

'I can see hilltops ahead,' said Een, excited.

Ali cheered up and said, 'Cool! Earth's HILL STATIONS are awesome. Finally, we will have fresh, clean air to breathe.'

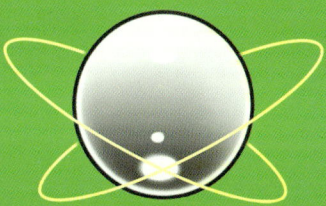

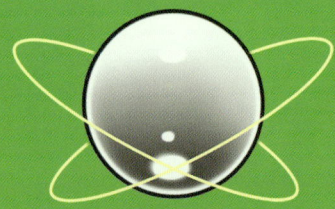

Soon they landed on top of a hill. But the moment they opened the dome of the spaceship and stepped out, they came across another horror.

'Aeeeooow! This is not a hill station but a FILTHY STINKING GARBAGE LANDFILL,' yelled Een, disgusted.

'Yuck! The smell is awful!' cried Ali and quickly they went inside their spaceship.

'I don't know how the humans can stay so close to these stinking dumps,' wondered Ali as he caught sight of a housing colony nearby.

As they moved towards the housing colony, they saw garbage trucks that stopped at intervals in the colony to collect garbage. This time they were disappointed to see the amount of mixed garbage that came out from each house. The same got dumped at the landfill.

'The humans are polluting the very air that they breathe!' exclaimed Ali, disgusted.

'Why can't they separate the WET waste from the DRY waste and RECYCLE it?' added Een.

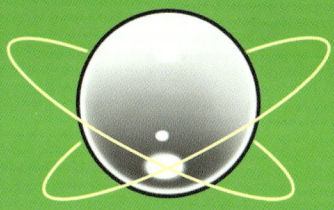

CHOP! CHOP! CHOP!

Suddenly a disturbing sound alerted Ali and Een. They followed it to find what they feared was the source of the sound. Trees, in a large area, were being cut down to built a housing society. They were shocked to see the placard that advertised the upcoming society.

'Don't they know that TREES breathe in dirty air and give out clean fresh air?' said Een, worried.

Feeling low, Ali said, 'This trip was a total waste. We came all this way for nothing. Let's go back.'

Een tried to pep him up, and said, 'Do not give up so soon, Ali. We will surely find a nice place to enjoy our holiday. A lot on Earth is left to be explored.'

Ali smiled hopefully as Een steered the spaceship over Earth. They kept scouting for some time for a place to land on but were disappointed.

Ali sighed, 'There is hardly any place left that is CLEAN and GREEN.'

'Can't we do something to make these humans understand that they need to FIX the damage they have caused or is it too late?' continued Ali.

'No, it is not late,' said Een thoughtfully. 'Let's show the humans how they can BE THE CHANGE and save Earth.'

So, Ali and Een communicated with humans on Earth.

HELLO! People on Earth.
We come in peace.
Planet Earth is crying for HELP!
YOU can **BE THE CHANGE** and SAVE YOUR ONE AND ONLY HOME.

We will share some simple ideas with you.

Follow them and live in a POLLUTION-FREE world.

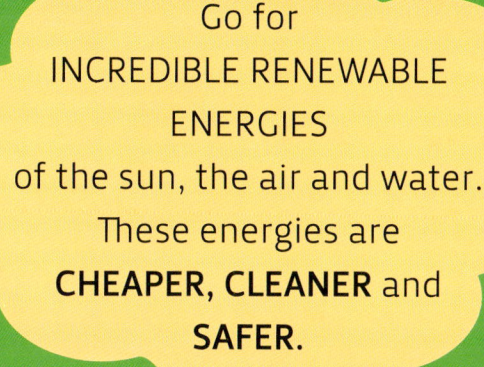

MIXED TRASH is STINKING TRASH.

SEGREGATED TRASH is CASH TRASH.

RIGHT ATTITUDE makes the EARTH HAPPY.

Your ONE and ONLY HOME.

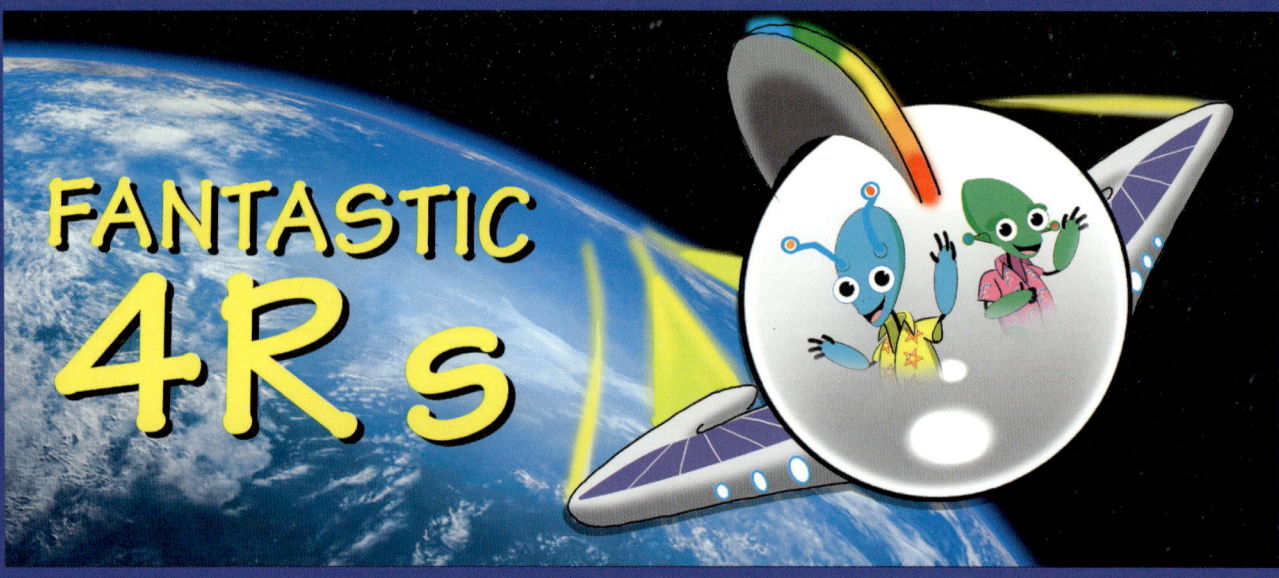

The people on Earth cheered for Ali and Een. They asked them to return in the near future to SEE the CHANGE on Earth and also to enjoy the holiday they never had. Ali and Een left with a parting message that said:

'Remember **4**, Remember **R**,
Together they become

The FANTASTIC 4Rs…
Reduce
Reuse
Recycle
Rethink.'